i

c

o

p

e

CCM Design by *Michael J Seidlinger*
Cover Design by *Olivia Croom*
Cover by *Wendy Ortiz*
ISBN - 978-1-937865-69-6

For more information, find CCM at:

http://copingmechanisms.net

BRUJA

a dreamoir

WENDY
C. ORTIZ

Dreamoir—a narrative derived from the most malleable and revelatory details of one's dreams, catalogued in bold detail. A literary adventure through the boundaries of memoir, where the self is viewed from a position anchored into the deepest recesses of the mind.

APRIL

I have an apartment, a small one, in downtown Los Angeles.
And guess who lives with me?

Jon, the guitarist from C Average.

This makes me very happy, albeit a bit confused.

The large bodies of water, an intense aquamarine blue, threw me off. I asked my host why they were so blue and he answered, *Well, what blue does it resemble?*

No words shaped in my head.

Turquoise, he answered himself, just as the word formed in my body.

Nicholas left the guesthouse we were staying in. I hurled my keys across the room. My hosts witnessed this act, and a veil of guilt fell over me.

While I looked around for Nicholas, I listened to conversations that my hosts were having. None seemed interesting to me.

I went to a whorehouse on my bike, Nicholas said when he entered the guesthouse.

I felt sixteen again. My rage curdled, emptied out into the room. I yelled until I became silent, withdrew from him. Something we were both used to.

The library had been converted into a house with a comfortable couch in its center. Thomas came to say goodbye to me. I looked around and saw my boss nearby. After all, I was at work.

Thomas began to kiss me. We moved to the couch, tongues entwined, my boss nearby. I formed the excuse in my head. *I'll just work later. She won't mind.*

"I think it would be a good idea if you let someone else do the next issue of *4th Street*," Thomas said when he came up for air. He said it so nonchalantly, stated it as fact. There was no anger, no menace in his mouth. I heard in his voice that I had no choice in this matter. It had been his literary journal.

No, Thomas, that can't be. I want to do it, I said weakly.

Thomas kissed me again. He held firm. "I think it would be best."

I thought his decision was an odd one, but held the information quietly, confused, my anger not quite awakened.

The protest was near UCLA. I saw Ren, caught his eye, waved, and said I'd be right back.

I did not go back to him.

I hiked to a car filled with people from my elementary and junior high schools. Queena was at the wheel. Mike, Brandon and others were squeezed into the VW convertible.

Queena drove like a banshee. She shot us over rooftops, let us hover over train tracks, sped next to rows of quiet houses. I closed my eyes when it felt reckless.

She successfully landed at her house and invited us in. Queena had done well for herself after junior high. In the first well-lit room she led us into, I heard, then saw, a little bird in the corner.

I decided that yes, I would have the baby.

Only one month along, I walked around unfamiliar streets and considered that there were already subtle changes going on in my body. I looked for people to share my news with, and clothes for the baby.

"I'm having a baby," I said to my father. He nodded, patted my shoulder. I took this as a sign of approval. I held open the bag of clothes my mother had saved, the clothes I wore as a baby. My father's face softened, and I saw it—he was impressed, impressed that my mother had saved the clothes, and impressed I would now be putting them to use.

As I took each piece of clothing out of the bag and unfolded it to look at it, I kept coming across smaller and smaller clothes, 70s fashions made for tiny baby bodies. I refolded them and put them back in the bag.

I decided to phone Tara, to tell her the news.

"This is Spencer," the voice on the other end told me. "Can I take a message? She's next door."

I left a message for Tara to call me, not believing she would, but bursting with the news. I wanted her to tell me it was alright, that I was making a good decision.

Later, the little blond boy I was taking care of tried every last drop of my patience. I wasn't sure he was mine, but it was my responsibility to watch him. And so I had to make an issue of the honey box.

"Please don't drink out of that box," I said, and picked him up and moved him far away from the honey.

The phone rang. I picked it up and heard Curt's voice. *Hello*, he said.

Hello, I said. My voice was muffled by congestion, as if I had a cold I was unaware of.

We went on talking, a very easy, casual conversation. I hid the excitement I felt deep inside me.

Driving the lumbering car through Los Angeles, I got pulled over by a female cop. Abigail and the other person in the car tensed in their seats. The cop told me to stay put before getting back into her black-and-white and rolling away.

Once she was out of sight I started my engine and drove a short distance. I threw open the door and ran inside the first building I saw. It was a halfway house. Panic flashed through my solar plexus. In the building across the street from me, men were silhouetted in the windows. I immediately figured it for a jail.

The cop never returned.

My therapist made a house call.

She walked into my childhood bedroom. My single bed was against the south wall of the room, where I like it to be in the summertime. She stood next to the bed while I talked. My obsession, my confusion took over the next hour.

When my time was up I got out of bed and accompanied my therapist to an auditorium. The interior resembled a barnyard. My therapist and I watched animals do tricks. People threw food and other objects at the animals and they caught every scrap in their mouths. We danced with great vigor with people dressed as various team mascots.

I made up my mind to leave. My dancing was just not up to snuff.

The hide-a-bed was clearly decades old, but the blankets on it felt warm and satisfying. Curt and I lied underneath the covers in the garage at my mother's house. The garage had always been a scary place for me: it was where my father spent weekend hours fixing things, tools laid out on dirty shelves; where I watched my father box a punching bag, his muscles working; where I gathered handfuls of pellets to feed the koi; where a pin-up calendar lived that my eyes always wanted to fix on, but which I resolutely ignored during my forays into this male place.

I knew it was around 3 a.m. and that my mother would be waking up for work soon. I felt as though she might come in to the garage looking for her clothes, as though she might forget that her clothes were actually in the house in my old bedroom. I feared her seeing yet another strange man in my bed. I had made her endure Nicholas and then Ren sleeping over at her house, which messed with her pseudo-Christian beliefs.

I wore a flimsy tiny beige tank top that I had carried around too long, worn through my teenage years into my late twenties. The cream-color of it was due to the organic cotton. It was peppered with tiny holes. At some point I had cut it in half attempting to make it a crop top. My near-nakedness made me slightly uncomfortable whenever I considered that my mother might walk in, looking for her own clothes. I was glad I had underwear on.

Curt alternately wore nothing (this I could feel under my fingertips, as they timidly touched his hip, his thigh, as he faced away from me) or two pairs of boxer shorts, both brightly colored.

Why are you wearing two pairs of boxer shorts? I asked. He was standing next to the bed, and I wanted him back in.

Why are you asking?

Because Michael wears two pairs of underwear, I lied. I had only wanted to say Michael's name in this garage.

Curt shrugged, got back into bed, straddled me playfully. I pulled the blankets around him so that my mother might not see some man's naked back and colorful boxer shorts.

Sleep never came. I monitored the internal clock. I lay next to Curt, who may or may not have been sleeping, and let my hands glide over his body, never touching with too much pressure, wanting to hide my desire. He let me touch him, rarely responded, and when he did, I was in a state of near-sleep, watching him through half-closed eyelids, willing my limbs to wrap around him, but my limbs would not listen. I had to be satisfied with this ghost dance in the curious bed, in my father's garage.

MAY

Two skunks. I petted one and I was not afraid at all that its tail was up.

I was told to choose a knife from the kitchen drawer, and my opponent would enter shortly.

I pulled open a drawer in this unfamiliar kitchen and chose two knives—the serrated one I walked outside with. My mother opened the screen door for me.

Once the knife was concealed in the gutter of a reachable roof next door, I hurried back inside. I held the butcher knife in my right hand the entire time.

My opponent was wheeled in.

He was blindfolded, but I knew this would come off when all the men in the room decided it would come off. His wheelchair had once been mangled then refurbished. I reminded myself I was probably seeing rust on it and not dried blood.

My mother faced me and I caught a scent of helplessness. Every muscle in my body became tense, constricted.

Then it hit me. My body quaked with sobs.

I don't want my mother to see me die, I said, and the blindfold came off the man's face.

I saw nothing.

When I awoke, the electricity was out, shelves of books had fallen, pieces of ceiling tile hung loose.

The air was not circulating.

I looked around, embarrassed that I might have fallen asleep at work. When I finally got the courage to walk through some of the rubble around my desk and ask someone if I'd fallen asleep, just as the words came out of my mouth, I realized we had all gone unconscious, that the power of the earthquake was like that of an explosion. Black burn marks tattooed the carpet and ceilings. We'd been knocked about like toys into unconsciousness.

I rubbed my eyes. This was a major catastrophic event. Injuries. Sirens.

It was five o'clock, but I wasn't sure I was going home.

JUNE

My mission was half-complete, but now I had to traverse a lake with black dolphins cavorting around me.

My fear trickled away.

These were secure waters, safe—unlike my mission.

Alligators surrounded us. Why had I let that person get me all the way out into the water? In the distance I spied pockets of land, dry sand, which I would need to use as stepping stones to stay out of the way of these creatures. They billowed up from the depths like breaching whales and smashed their scaly bodies against each other. They looked to be a thousand pounds each and caused great splashes.

I let two people, sweet people I know and trust on an acquaintance level, pick me up, one supporting me under each armpit, and I was carried to safety, past the alligators, and out of the water. Out of danger.

I stood in my apartment.

My boyfriend, looking like Iggy Pop, long and lanky with black hair and blue eyes, stood in the room with me, his black clothes contrasting nicely with my light blue carpet. The south wall of the room was glass, two large windows open like sliding glass doors, with no screens.

A skunk jumped in through one window, crossed the carpet, and jumped out the other window. I barely had time to stand back and freeze, fearful of its spray, the scent of which I normally love, but only when it's carried in on the wind. Before I could recover, a possum tumbled in, and chasing it was a cheetah, right in through the first window, right out the second window.

I was astonished. This was for sure a lucky sighting.

JULY

The woman in charge of showing me a series of slides had long honey-blond hair.

You'll be watching a bear, she said.

As I watched in earnest, I noticed that there was sound and movement. One bear whispered into the ear of another. The one being whispered to spoke and the voice was the voice of the woman showing me the slide.

I shifted in my seat uncomfortably.

I packed my bags at least three times. I was booked on a trip to New York but I wondered if I would ever make it because the damn bags needed to be packed and unpacked and packed again.

Abigail, others I knew from school, some strangers, and I milled around a beach house.

The ocean waves were clearly getting bigger and as I went to close the door I heard myself say, *How close do these waves usually get?* just as the foam reached the patio. I hardly had time to close both doors in the high winds when another huge wave rumbled toward the house. The wind blew the doors open again.

I climbed up on top of an armoire, yelling to others to stand on couches and other furniture, and most important, to *Hang on*. The water crashed through the living room and out again.

Moments later, the ocean went still, without a ripple.

I showed AQ that Sh. had written a book. I was listed on the acknowledgments page.

As my finger slid down the fine print, through all the sources he had reprinted from, I noticed he had created his own press.

"you!" press it was called.

I skimmed through an additional scene from a play, also on the acknowledgments page—the only character I recall being "Queen"—and closed the book.

I had never known Sh. to be a writer.

I took a night hike with an enormous group of people spanning my entire life.

We trampled on big crackly leaves like it was autumn in the Pacific Northwest.

Rounding out a smooth brown hill I wanted to call a mountain but knew its size would not allow it that, I realized I had to circle it down, down, down to get to my belongings and leave this place.

I looked forward to the descent.

AUGUST

I drove a black truck to visit Olympia. I had cats with me. I parked outside the garage of the first place I ever mud-wrestled and when I opened the door of the truck, the cats kind of spilled out. The cats weren't mine and I panicked.

After unloading some containers of spoiled food (pasta, fruit, lentils), a bunch of cats caroused all around my feet. I was overwhelmed trying to figure out which one was the one I was missing. Some had little tiny slips of paper on the napes of their necks, where you hold them when you want them to submit to the power of the mother cat. I saw numbers and some lettering on them, but none of it told me which cat was which. They all looked exactly alike.

When I found the right one, I got him into the truck cab while all the others continued brushing against my feet and calves.

Hiking, camping. Packing of bags. A small lodge that I had grown accustomed to and had to leave. I was amazed at my backpack and how long I had been out in the wilderness like this.

The aboveground pool held our bodies in its cavernous deep. Everyone at the hotel had access to it. I held onto the concrete edges and pushed myself up and down in the water while I watched a little boy get very close to a dolphin (though someone called it a whale) that sped around in our midst, coming up near us, then plunging into the deep again.

When the animal next surfaced, I saw it was indeed a small whale. A huge sea turtle lunged out of the water. The little boy threw himself at its shell playfully. I got angry. He acted as though this sea turtle was a toy.

I swam around the edges of the pool looking for the boy's parents. They were drinking champagne even though it was morning. They looked pale, groggy, overdressed. They barely paid any attention to me as I calmly suggested that they teach their son not to play rough with the animals. I swam away when I realized they weren't listening.

The pool changed shape altogether, became shallower, with no animals. A television was perched up in the corner of the gym-like room. The host of a local talk show announced that they would be doing a show on 'excommunication'— which referred to excommunications from art groups.

I smiled to myself and did laps.

People around the pool began to get up and leave.

Someone from school I didn't know well called out to me, "Are you coming?"

I'm already an expert in being excommunicated! I cried out, almost laughing.

I moved from the pool to a rented room with a large bed where I reclined. I held the remote and surfed channels. Ren was there. He looked older, staid, dressed conservatively. He was seducing me as usual.

I couldn't get past his attire. While we made the motions of foreplay, I wondered about why he had completely changed his look.

I wasn't sure I liked it.

I was the pallbearer. The body was contained in identical gift boxes, each the size of a watch box.

My job was to put the body in order.

As I worked, I noticed: a box etched with the number eight, a box etched with a rose.

The doctor, a petite Chinese woman, arranged her tools as I awaited surgery.

There were three silver trays: in one, something like cooked spinach sat in water. In the second, a healing salve that looked like green gelatin and which I knew would feel like menthol. The third tray had sharp incision-making instruments.

I lay on the table, scared, knowing I would only be getting a local anesthetic. My belly was exposed. I was anxious: she might cut into my appendectomy scar.

Adrenaline coursed through me.

When she began making a long incision in the area next to my big toe, cutting down into the top of my foot and I did not feel a thing, my body flushed hot with relief.

Fake rocks outlined the perimeter of the shallow pool. I stood in a circle with many others, here for the same purpose, as we watched a shark swimming, gliding between the farthest reaches of the circle.

Panic rushed through me every time the shark went near someone. Then it came to me.

There was nowhere to go so I let it bite me.

The shark grabbed onto my foot with its teeth.

The pain was excruciating. I worried over the broken bones and flesh. I dissolved into the pain.

When I awoke in the back of my mother's old station wagon, my first thought was that I hoped I was being taken to a hospital, or somewhere far from more danger.

When I looked at my foot, there were only red marks where teeth had been. My skin was smooth, without puncture, unwounded.

I sat at a computer. The website I was looking at was comprised of articles about Israel. I waited for two links to articles about Palestine to open. Every time I clicked on the links, the articles opened, but they were the wrong articles. They were articles about Israel.

Finally, the links changed, and I found the two articles about Palestine.

One of my colleagues was making the rounds, hugging and kissing all of us goodbye. When she got to me, she held my face in her hands and compared us to a historical duo, names I don't remember, but names that connote two women known for their strength.

She moved on to the next colleague and kissed her excessively as the recipient kept trying to get away to go teach a class. I was hot with discomfort.

SEPTEMBER

Someone gave me an absolutely perfect, spotless, white, old-fashioned, lace-up pair of roller skates.
They fit me.
I pulled them on, pleased as punch.

Everyone around me was on LSD or shrooms. Hundreds of people played a very involved-looking game. There were strangely folded papers with clues, the paper like college-ruled notebook paper, laced with pen scrawls.

Young men took running leaps and scaled the sides of buildings up to three stories high before they tumbled back down onto the grass and did it again.

I got upset with someone for not explaining the elaborate game to me. I met Queena on the swing, a very intricate swing/pulley system that we used to get from floor to floor of the open-air party house several stories tall. In talking with her, I learned that Queena was a hardcore drug user, a piece of information that more than surprised me.

I was a queen.

I wore a thick velvet and brocade dress of black and burgundy.

My husband was king. He looked like Aragorn from the movie "Lord of the Rings." His name was Agarwal. I was wrenched away from him.

Men dragged me by my dress across the palace floor, screaming, *Agarwaaaaaaaaaal!* I moaned long moans that stretched out into sobs as he was being pulled away from me, his arms failing to reach mine.

The long pulling cries and sobs took up residence in my chest. I feared they would get stuck there, never leave.

S. and I lived together in my childhood bedroom. Sunlight streamed in through the blinds.

We hosted a huge party on the hardwood floors of the house.

I opened my closet and most of my clothes were missing. In my rummaging I found a very cool dress, white and full, with one scratchy petticoat sewed into it. The bodice had purple and pink dots.

Coyly, I said to S., *Want me to wear this?*

Reclined across the bed, he grinned at me. I held up the bottom of the dress and caressed the roughness of the petticoat. I rubbed the edge across his lips.

C. invited me over to his apartment in Seattle. I could tell he was very excited about something, and then he burst out that he and his girlfriend were moving in together.

Suddenly I was a fly on the wall in their bathroom.

I watched his new girlfriend come in. She shut the door and began to tremble. Her eyes rolled back, and she started crying, a scary rage-filled lament, though she barely a sound.

Hmmm, I wondered, rubbing my legs together. *Does C. know about this?*

I was in a place that was supposed to be Olympia, Washington.

It had more public transportation, including electric buses.

I tried to keep hold of a cat that belonged to Michael. It was orange and white and looked something like the thin orange and white short-hair tabby I had when I was in junior high. I knew the cat was on one of the buses and actually saw it inside when one bus went by and the door opened. The cat was on its back, holding onto a lowered handle-like bar near the floor, acting like it was a performer, or on an amusement park ride. I ran after the bus.

When I finally just stood near a bus stop and called for the cat, it flew off the bus and ran toward me. I took it to Michael's house and fed it, but then realized I was using the wrong bowls for its food and water. I had to clean the bowls out and start over.

My father and I and my adopted family took a road trip. We drove alongside a lake that was in the middle of transforming into an ocean. A tidal wave was coming at us. When our car floated gently right at the surface, we all laughed, marveling at how this could be so.

My father and I stood near the lake. I was on the sandy shore while my father stood above me on rocks. We admired the seals in the water. I blew a kiss at one and her pup. The pup came flopping and gliding over to me on the shore. It practically jumped into my arms, so I cuddled it. Ecstatic, I held up the pup so my dad would see. He was holding one, too.

After I'd let the pup back into the water, all the seals vanished.

The lake became see-through and weirdly still. My father waded into the lake with me until we were both knee-high in water. Two huge shadows moved toward us and I realized they were sharks. We scrambled out of the water, struggling for higher ground. I hesitated to turn toward the water, sure I would see a mouthful of jagged teeth right behind me.

When I reached a higher clearing of rocks that was still too close to the water for comfort, I saw AQ. She was investigating the wide-open mouth of an alligator with a huge magnifying glass. She looked very intent, oblivious to my shock. Some people had gathered around her, all of us mystified.

Suddenly the alligator's mouth snapped shut and her magnifying glass went *crack* but she was fine.

A television show about artists held my complete focus in my mother's living room, despite all the unfamiliar men, also in the living room, who were focused on me.

The show was about two particular artists. They wore wild and colorful clothes. No one but me seemed interested, so people in the room talked about where they lived. An unfamiliar older woman I hadn't seen earlier asked me where I lived.

In seedy, dirty Hollywood, and I love it, I said, enjoying every word.

OCTOBER

A big dark house surrounded by a grove of weeping willow trees. I lived there and loved it.

I noticed my cat in the room. I was pleased she was with me. Out of the corner of my eye I saw other moving, furry things. They became cats, scuttling all over the floor, along with a big fluffy rabbit. Everything was squirmy underfoot. I was unnerved even as much as I wanted to laugh.

At the wedding ceremony, I was a guest along with many other women I was only vaguely familiar with, as familiar as I felt with the women being married to one another.

Guests sat on barstools. It was ten to six, and I knew I would be married to S. at six. I still needed to get over to the houseboat, and in the back of my head, I knew I would have to decide which houseboat to be married on. When I thought about it, I knew everyone would like the one named *Pretty Pretty* but I hated its bland, cutesy décor—fake blond wood paneling, little country flower stencils on white walls.

All through the other wedding ceremony I felt ill. I knew I could not be married. It would go against everything I had ever stood for. I also knew that if I decided not to, I would be disappointing many people, mostly S. and my mom, right at the last minute.

S. waited back at the houseboats as I worked these things out in my head.

I took my mother aside and told her I couldn't do it. We got into a yelling match in front of the all the other wedding's guests. I repeatedly used my foot for emphasis: "No, I cannot go through with this." *Stamp.*

I looked into my mother's eyes—she was enraged I was pulling out—and yelled, "Bring it on!"

Then: "Well, I could have a commitment ceremony,

just not a marriage by law."

This seemed to put everyone a little more at ease.

By then it was five to six. I still had to get back to the house-boat and get into my dress and tell S. we could not be married by law, but we could have a commitment ceremony instead.

I could hardly believe I had gone even this far from my principles, that I had been about to be married. Relief washed over me when I realized I could walk away.

I re-met Sh. after a year hiatus.

We, in fact, reunited.

I had a party at my apartment, and he showed up. There was a misunderstanding or miscommunication in the air.

I felt the dread coming on.

He broke up with me, and though I didn't resist that, I thought, *No. Not another negative thing with you. Why? How could I have let this happen again?*

The melancholy swept me down.

Someone with the initials DP rained biochemical weapons down on us. The palm trees were bombarded. We wilted in the intense heat of the explosions.

I saw T.

She wore a small green t-shirt, kelly green, with green short-shorts. We were in a public place, a busy plaza full of people. She pushed a stroller.

We did not speak, though our eyes met briefly.

I was the mistress of a much older man. I walked down a crowded avenue to meet him, but could only hug him passionately once his wife had walked past us.

He was in his fifties, with a full head of thick black hair with lots of gray in it. He wore a button-down shirt and held a cardigan sweater under one arm. It was apparent he was wealthy. I understood he was a Mexican dignitary or politician.

When we hugged, it was all I could do to not melt into him. When I pulled away from him on the busy avenue I left a film of sadness in my wake.

Eloise told me of a writer's residency I should attend, but warned me about the snakes on the way.

"If you can get past the snakes, you'll be fine," she said.

I took a forest path that shifted from light to dark. The trees stood tall and skinny with white trunks, their branches blotting out the sky.

The path became a very tight ledge and I held onto the interlocking branches I found at eye level. Some of the branches, mossy and green, were not branches at all, but green snakes. Their heads stuck out in the few open spaces, still and waiting.

I jumped off the ledge. The sun shone where I landed. I found a residence hall and saw Eloise. I interrupted her conversation to tell her that unfortunately there was no way I could get past those snakes. She seemed bothered by my presence, so I turned to leave.

A Green Tortoise bus pulled up. Hippie-looking people tumbled off of it.

I walked past them, back into the forest.

Six of us, most in Halloween costumes, marched through neighborhoods. We were promoting acceptance of mixed-race marriages and families.

No one spoke to me so I mostly watched and listened. One man was in a costume of a man and by the end of the march I finally figured out from all of his negative, bitter comments that he was a twentysomething white man, and he was feeling very guilty.

We ended up in a U-shaped plaza. On one side was a biker bar, but it looked from the outside like an innocuous kind of place you'd find in a bland, boring part of town; the other side had an ice cream shop. The silver bike under my hands belonged to Frank. I set it next to me while I talked to Barbara and Tasch and told them about the march. Minutes later, the bike was gone. They hadn't noticed me walking it so I didn't mention it. I wandered around the plaza casually scanning for it, my heart sinking.

When I saw Frank again he was carrying an enormous painting of big, green, veiny leaves on a rich black background. At the bottom was a woman with a lifelike heart. Abigail and I stood on either side of the painting and Frank held it by the frame between us. I held a soft rag that, when lightly rubbed into the painting, completely erased the image until it was a white canvas. The rubbing motion was relaxing, simple.

I stood on the stepstool in the kitchen of the house in the forest.

People milled about. Someone pointed out all the real wood paneling.

I opened all the cupboards I could reach. They contained very old glass jars of spice. In one cupboard I found a small glass enclosure full of ancient cupcake sprinkles.

I poured the contents of every jar I opened into the wastebasket next to the stepstool.

When I arrived at my childhood home that night, there was a message from my mother that she would not be coming home. It sounded slightly cryptic and made me sad. She seemed to indicate she was staying with someone and that she thought it was time I lived alone anyway.

In the morning I went to look around and in the patio my father struggled with the carpet. He was resigned that my mother had left, too. I didn't want to discuss it with him. I figured he had a hand in driving her away from me. In fact, he repelled me.

When I saw her again I felt steeled against her.

My mother used an unfamiliar soothing voice to speak to me, but seemed very focused on her own experience, not caring that she had left me alone in the house. Anger and resentment brewed in me as I imagined returning to the same house, with its three bedrooms, night after night, alone.

It was daytime and I was murdering my mother.

I had knives, guns and a cat o' nine tails at my disposal. The only other person there was not trying to stop me, and neither was my mother. My blood was hot with the threat of something. I only knew this: I had to defend.

I plunged the largest knife into her chest over and over. She would not die.

I felt bone against the knife. Disgust like a smell that wouldn't leave my nose. I pulled the knife out of her body. Again. Again.

My slow murder of her happened all over the house. We landed on the porch. It felt like hours, with only the noise of my torture, our heavy breathing and gasps.

Finally, I used the cat o' nine tails on her head. Each swing was a miss.

She urged me on. I paused for a moment.

There was something to the fact of her urging me.

There was a reason I had to kill her and she wanted me to.

I swung the instrument twice, each time bashing her forehead. Her face turned ashen, then green, and she fell against the front step.

Terrified, sad, relieved, disgusted, I wondered what this would mean.

I checked her to make sure she was dead. She smiled

even in death.

I stepped over her and into the house.

DECEMBER

Someone threw me a birthday party. Dozens of people milled around the unfamiliar kitchen and den.

The party took place in Washington state. There was a long drive to get to the lake. We had abandoned the pizza parlor idea. Mariella drove me in a glittery red golf cart to the edge of the water. Many of the picnic tables were already taken and I wondered when all my guests would arrive.

I squealed and pointed out a large black fish in the lake to Mariella. The fish swam fast, forming perfect arcs as they tossed themselves out of the water. Meanwhile, strangers took all the remaining picnic tables. I was powerless to reserve any when there were only two of us, even though I knew the party would be huge.

I saw my people marching toward us from a faraway parking lot. There'd be no tables for them.

I returned to the house. The party had not started; everyone was out, I assumed, getting food and drinks to bring. I understood that everyone was on a second trip to get party supplies. My frustration grew as it got later and later.

My mother walked through the doorway into the kitchen

and though she was in her twenties, her face looked puffy and her hair disheveled. I was incensed that everyone had left, and before they'd gone, they had drunk all the beer without offering me any on my birthday. I pushed and threw punches at my mother. She mostly surrendered.

Next I got into a fistfight with Abigail. She was alternately wobbly, as if drunk, then upright and ferocious as we fought. When my contact lens popped out of one eye she tried to scratch it off my face. Without saying so, we took a time-out, panting, while I popped the lens back into my eye and resumed fighting.

Our altercation over, with no clear winner, we had a conversation about how nice her legs were.

"Does your boyfriend ever tell you so?" I asked. She told me he used to, but not so much anymore.

"They seem so long, so strong," I said. Her legs reminded me of horses.

Once again in the Olympia-that-is-not-Olympia.

I walked into a motel room in a walk-up brick building to be with Ren.

He was not smiling.

We had sex, which felt uneventful, and then he practically spat at me, angered. Then silence.

"If you feel this way, why did you even have sex with me?"

He glared in reply.

Outraged, I took his suitcase and pulled one item at a time out of it, throwing each piece with much aplomb into the hallway of the motel, yelling about his attitude, his fucked-up-ness, and so on.

I was surrounded by brindle-colored cats and dogs. I leaned down and hugged a dog-sized cat. Warmth enveloped me as I hugged this cat's neck and let my hands sink into her fur.

We were in a movie theater. I wore skirts with multi-colored petticoats, my hair long with multiple braids.

I shared a loveseat with Abigail and a few times our loveseat completely slid down the aisle to the front row of seats. We laughed, quieted ourselves, and pushed the loveseat back up to the top.

We drank milk—she, white milk; me, chocolate.

I was running late for a music show, missed my bus, contemplated running all the way there (I felt as though I would bound like a gazelle and could make it, no problem) but I ended up getting on a bus. When I got home, where I meant to change my clothes, there was only an hour left before the performance. It was 8 p.m. and the sun shone like a jewel.

The little boy returned.

He was around two years old with blond hair. He was wiggly and warm.

We readied to go to Disneyland with my adopted family. D. asked several times if I liked her new style, which was loud, brash, and risqué. I said more than once that I loved it, that I loved her, and that I had missed her.

I knew the little boy was my son.

JANUARY

I wore a red negligee and had an invisible sheet that functioned as a magic carpet. If in flight I flapped it just once, I went higher and higher in the sky.

Eventually I landed on a brick wall behind a liquor store. A bunch of men were standing around outside of an old truck, leering at me. I pretended I didn't see them and went inside.

I was pregnant. Had been for about seven months. I wasn't showing and was afraid S. would know. The thought depressed me. Here I was, seven months pregnant, drinking alcohol, smoking, flying, and hadn't seen a doctor the entire time.

My belly was firm.

Prostitutes, phone sex operators, and strippers were my hosts, and I the guest.

Everyone was sweet and kind. We became friendly and I was accepted as part of their large household.

I became romantically linked with a close friend of theirs named David Shelton. He was tall, thin, lanky, with blond hair and glasses. He spoke in a low voice. I was thrilled every time we were alone.

The women in the house looked on and smiled at our romantic entanglement.

The filmmaker Michael Moore, Veronica, and I were on a road trip. At one of our stops, three rabid dog-wolves surrounded us on a dirt playground.

I learned that I had to be very quiet and move slowly, if at all, to get the animals to move away and pay attention to something else.

I left the supermarket after dark. It was cold. Someone bundled up in a coat, scarf, and hat said my name. He told me it was okay, he knew I was shopping at Ralph's, and he'd forgive me. It was one of my mentors, and he was being sarcastic, yet I still felt incredibly guilty for having been caught shopping at Ralph's, whose workers were still locked out of their jobs.

The fairgrounds were big, dusty. Long winding paths lead to the parking lots that were just as big and dusty. The sun beat down on us. While walking one of the paths, I started to leap. With each leap, I went higher and higher until I soared hundreds of feet in the air, traversing about one hundred yards ahead on the path when I landed.

On the descent I feel the slight pull in my stomach, the breath leaving my chest, coupled with exhilaration.

S. and I sat on the floor of a small music venue. I had my fluffy blue slippers on and felt slightly self-conscious.

A lot of Olympia girl bands were scheduled to play and there were familiar people in the audience. S. told me he'd be following one of the bands on tour the following week. I was shocked at how little notice he gave me that he was going on the road.

"Well, if you're going to do that, then I get to go out on dates with other people while you're gone," I said.

Our conversation was cut short by the sound of raucous drums coming from the back of the room. I wanted to leave, but it was too late. We listened to the drums and guitars. I fumed inwardly.

FEBRUARY

I had an affair with Governor Arnold Schwarzenegger.

We sat in my childhood bedroom calmly discussing our plans to marry once he had divorced his present wife. He was not yet inaugurated state governor.

Me: submissive. Him: patronizing.

At the inauguration ceremony, held in a park, I stood atop the last row of bleachers. From this vantage point, I could see the choreographed men in suits skipping and dancing from four corners of the park. Many of them were grown men with whom I had gone to elementary school. Their faces were covered in white make-up.

I moved closer to the front row of bleacher seats. I wanted the governor to be able to see me from the podium. He entered the area with his wife. I felt no jealousy or doubt. I knew we would be married once their divorce was final.

Different people I knew were shocked at this turn of events.

In many of our conversations, I was asked how I could marry a Republican. I was very sincere and adamant: I too could hardly believe I would be marrying a Republican, but just think: I would be the wife of the governor and could therefore start all kinds of beneficial programs and be of help in that capacity.

Everyone still seemed shocked.

In the face of their shock, I felt calm and complacent about my decision.

The flammable man and I rode a train on a half-day trip. We sat across from each other. I could see the coastline through the windows.

We talked a lot and eventually began kissing. I stopped us both. "I have a boyfriend," I said, by way of reminder.

We paused momentarily and though we made out off and on afterward, the mood had changed. I felt pretty sure that everything would be different once we got off the train.

I found my way to a rental car after having been deposited somewhere in Agoura or Calabasas: lots of yellow and brown hills, the air dry and warm. I asked people for help, got rides, passed Rinaldi Street, but I did not have an address or directions of where to go.

Eventually a Greyhound bus took me to Olympia. It took only six hours to get there.

When I arrived, Michael was living in a house in the middle of a field. I walked across the field in pouring rain toward the front door. Young men were tooling around with something I couldn't see, then running. I heard Michael's voice. He yelled at me to run.

I ran toward the front door, altering my trajectory a bit since I had my head down. There was an explosion and I jumped through the threshold.

Michael explained that the men were practicing detonating bombs.

Cats filled the house. When I looked around, I saw women I didn't recognize among the cats, but none of the cats was our cat. I started to panic, moving faster through the house, calling my cat's name, and occasionally a cat would appear perched on my shoulder or draped over my arm, but none of them mine.

In the backyard, a collection of cats dozed on lawn chairs. One of them was mine. I was relieved, almost crying, and amazed that she had dozed through all the noise of detonating bombs. Why was Michael living near this mayhem? How could our cat stand it?

She had her collar on, with her name and Michael's phone number. She sat still while I pressed my forehead against her fur.

I found an invisible button and pushed it.

Everything—*everything*—turned white. A complete blank white slate, no forms, shadows, dimensions.

It reminded me of Bugs Bunny cartoons when the animator showed up and erased the backgrounds around the characters, then erased the characters.

The professor of my philosophy class was about thirty-five, very talkative, inquisitive, and moved all around the class-room as he spoke. He had wavy grayish/blondish hair that hit his shoulders. He was dressed very informally.

At one point he directed his lecture at me and to make his point he came up very close to me, touching me in a way that was inappropriate, yet humorous.

Later during his lecture, he sidled up to me. I confided in him that it had been years since I was an undergraduate and I had no experience with a traditional classroom setting. I was used to seminars and interdisciplinary programs at liberal arts colleges.

What I didn't tell him was that I hadn't minded when he touched me.

We rode the trolley backward.

The little girl next to me looked like me when I was small.

She wore a frilly white dress and little white shoes. We listened to a broadcast—an NPR game show, by the sounds of it.

We each had clipboards with paper. There were illustrations of different kinds of bread, given to us as clues. I wrote:

challah
egg bread

When unsure of the answers, I wrote down keywords that might be related to the clue.

I glanced at the little girl's clipboard. She could write, too.

MARCH

I stood inside my fifth floor apartment in the tall brick building. My window was open and it was afternoon. Four young men were running along rooftops toward my apartment. One of the men flung three sticks of dynamite, bound together with one fuse, into my open window.

I panicked, and the other person in the apartment with me grew alarmed and I yelled, *Run!* Off we dashed. I wanted to bang on all the doors of the apartments on our way down but I had little to no energy in my arm. When I tried to pound my fist against one, it came out as a light knock, barely a tap. I yelled at invisible tenants to get out of the building. I ran into no one on the way down.

From a block away I watched the building explode.

The detail of the side of the building that had been my apartment fell into itself, collapsing, crumbling down, a straight line that transformed into a cloud of dust.

I thought of the writing left behind in that apartment, and how I had lost it all.

Roscoe Boulevard. Dusk. I was heading home.

A man, naked except for camouflage paint covering his body, jumped out of a manhole on my route. A moment later, two other men, who I thought were law enforcement, came over and began beating him.

When I realized they were not law enforcement I felt a little strange. Who were they? Who leaped out of the manhole? What led to this situation?

I guided my car onto the 170 Freeway, away from the scene.

I decided to go out with Sh. again, because he asked me. I felt prickly with distrust, but I went anyway. His brother, another blond man, accompanied us.

His brother did all the talking. I was pretty certain he didn't know that Sh. and I had a history.

I sat quietly in the passenger seat and snuck glances at Sh., who was nearly silent. His hair had grown out a little, and he was taller and slimmer.

We went to Julie and Bill's house. On the big grassy slope in front of the house, we got sidetracked by a game. Someone handed me a baby. I felt good holding the baby. Sh. came close to me, but still nothing of substance had been said yet. People on the grassy slope suggested places for us to go, and we—me, Sh., his brother—got back into Sh.'s black car and went to a coffeehouse.

In the coffeehouse, a group of people sat around on the floor and in the few scattered chairs. I didn't know if Sh. had broken up with his girlfriend. Or if this was a date.

Finally, Sh. said something to me from across the room. The something he said put a face on our conflict, for all of these strangers to hear. Although stunned, I replied.

As I waited for a response, I could tell the group around us was growing uneasy, as if my reply was too hard on Sh.

C. was next to me, so I whispered, *This is exactly what*

it was like dating this guy, this waiting, these weird comments, this conflict just under the surface, and *What the fuck am I doing on a date with him now?*

Sh.'s brother broke in and told me Sh. was just that way, to not take it personally. I responded a little too loudly. *Yeah, right. That's exactly why we broke up.*

I felt like I could make a clean getaway. I asked C. if she could give me a ride home.

Sh. called my name. Against my better judgment, I turned. Suddenly he was holding me in his arms and saying halfway apologetic things. I could feel C. waiting for me.

In a pseudo-gentle voice, I told him, *I'm not sure this would work, are you? Do you think you can be different this time, will you be able to be mature, and emotionally available?*

C. jingled her keys at me, like, *Let's go!*

There was no fear as the ten of us swam and bobbed in the ocean waves. It was sunset. The rhythmic bobbing felt soothing, sexual.

The sky darkened way too quickly and we found ourselves looking at dark, thick storm clouds in the sky. I stared and stared at a large hole with light coming through, deep in the middle of the black clouds. The circle of light was hypnotic, until I realized that the kind of clouds around it meant serious snow, and we had better get out of the water, fast.

There was all the scrambling and mild panic of trying to swim against the tide and get back to shore. We made it to the patio deck. S. ran around wearing a yellow tutu.

I met The One.

He was a little younger than me, Japanese, attentive, smart, and very good-looking. I can't remember his name. I discerned that it would be easy to tell him I was in a relationship already, but planned to leave it. I would be leaving it for him.

We were in a motel with bland twin beds. The attention The One gave me was courteous, almost courtly.

Then I understood: he was indeed courting me.

I began to imagine what our children might look like.

My grandmother walked faster than I had seen her walk in years.

I sat in a station wagon parked at a curb and watched her across the street, walking a small incline, swift. I was amazed. When she walked back to the car, she lit up a cigarette. I was almost as shocked by this as I was by her speed. She hadn't smoked in about 40 years.

I looked down at the business card of the man I was attracted to.

The words on his business card: *Clover Father*.

I was back in Olympia for a visit. I ended up at the place that is called the co-op but is nothing like the co-op.

I ran into Hali. I was glad to see her. We hung out for a while until I sighed and said, *It's been two weeks and I haven't even told Michael I'm in town yet.*

I was given a new keyboard.

The new keyboard was white and felt lighter than a normal computer keyboard.

I began to type on it but realized it was missing some buttons.

When I looked at my old keyboard to compare the two, there were four blank buttons situated in a little cluster on the right-hand side. I realized I wanted those buttons, even needed those buttons, so the new keyboard was rendered useless.

I didn't have my lines memorized. I lost my schedule of when I was supposed to be at rehearsals. I didn't know when I was supposed to arrive on opening night, and I was one of the stars of the play.

I had found out I was in the play only two nights before opening. Abigail was also in the play. She seemed to have the schedule. She was disappointed I didn't.

My father ran into Abigail's mom's car on the 170 freeway. Her family drove up and parked in front of my mother's house.

Everyone was very disappointed with my father. He hung his head but had a drunk smirk on his face. That pissed me off the most.

At my mother's house, monstrous disembodied hands reached through walls. I repeated the 23rd Psalm over and over.

Nothing stopped the scaly claws that reached into the bathroom, grabbing at me and the white cat.

AQ and I were in a department store admiring the same denim jacket. A beautiful blood-red flower adorned the back of the jacket.

I meandered around the department store, keeping my eye on the jacket.

When I saw my mother, she asked me a series of annoying questions until I burst out, *Can you stop asking me so many questions?*

AQ purchased the jacket. I called across the store to her to confirm. She held it in her grasp. When I went to the rack, there were no more like it left.

I decided to busy myself with looking for things that would be good for living in a camper. Travel items.

I looked at a display of C.'s photos in the department store and pointed them out to my mother. There were black and white prints of rocks in a forest, with animals on them: two rabbits (one I recognized as C.'s), mice, fireflies.

As we held a print, there was a snap of dust in the air and the animals began to twitch and move. We gasped in surprise and I laughed.

The United States had closed all of its borders.

I was in a hotel room when I found out, on the east coast, near the Canadian border.

There was a government man in a blue suit charged with calming large crowds of people. He told us that we could not leave the country and, in fact, we could not go anywhere but the immediate area.

The crowd protested amongst itself. We could not believe this turn of events. I said aloud, *Perhaps we can go underwater and declare water sovereign.* I was half-joking.

At the Canadian border, a woman read a prepared statement telling us why we could not cross. It was clear from the way she held her mouth tensely as she read that she had not written it herself.

A number of us in the crowd protested her outright. In the small swell of panic, I contemplated what I would do—set fires, burn my way out of the country.

In my grandmother's house on Euclid, I spoke to a group of people about how special Michael is to me, how I've cherished him in my life. A few moments later, Michael walked in the front door, smiling and unaware of my monologue about him.

S.'s friend Mike from the Bay area handed me a rat, sweet and calm, that reminded me of one of Ren's rats. I thought it was a strange gift, but I accepted.

I spied a coffin-looking container. Inside, I was told, was a half-eaten man. I watched as a crowd of overly large sewer rats fed on the body.

Ren and I reunited.

We stood around outside an unfamiliar cafe, reminiscing, coming together, holding one another, trying to be discreet about the feelings still between us while strangers looked on. Ren wore strange glasses like S.'s. He smoked cigarettes, which I found perplexing.

Abigail arrived and we frantically looked around for a place to be alone on the upper floor. Our hands were on each other's bodies when we weren't busy looking for a small space to be intimate. We didn't do a very good job of looking.

Melissa's boyfriend had murdered Melissa in the strange house.

I explained afterward that he was like a blank spot to me—I couldn't remember his face at all and therefore was not a good witness. N. leaned Melissa's body against a low brick wall amid our anxious sobbing. When the police arrived, we found that the body had already decomposed. Melissa's legs were separated from the rest of her body.

We were immediately thrust into war.

Abigail, Michael, a small tuxedo cat, a dog, and I made the decision to run into the fray together.

As we sprinted, I saw little boys throw Molotov cocktails. One boy set fire to an electrical wire that had fallen. We jumped low barricades and past flames, ran under live wires. The chaos followed.

Eventually, we found our shack, and with it, Melissa's body. Her body was like a costume of her skin, her face just a mask. Someone in the shack freaked out, said she never wanted to lay eyes on that thing again. I didn't want to get rid of Melissa's body, as it might be evidence, so I buried it under a pile of clothes and plastic dry-cleaning bags in a corner of the shack.

I was sad for the little cat that had accompanied us on our journey. She slept in deep exhaustion. I whistled her awake and tried to find scraps for her to eat. I was anxious at the thought of how little she was and how I was going to keep track of her or care for her. How I might lose her.

My mother and I rode a plane to the East Coast.

We sat in seats with nothing around us: the body of the aircraft, even down to the seats, was completely invisible.

I wondered how this would affect us, but no one else seemed concerned.

Later on the trip, I watched my adopted family play baseball in front of the cottage we were staying in. The view from the front porch was of dazzling snow-covered mountains. *If I could hike down into the valley and up the mountain, how long would it would take?* I wondered. From where I was I could see a hiker making their way up.

Back in the cottage, I was in charge of a toddler I didn't recognize.

My grandmother and I, along with three cats, sat in my mother's living room.

A number of adult cats crowded the patio. I started to count them. They were all different colors and relatively the same size. Each time I had a count going, a new cat appeared, and I began the count over.

Finally, I settled on 12 cats, 15 in all including those rubbing against our calves in the living room.

I parked my bicycle, heavy with bags, outside the front door of the large old house in Olympia. It was painted white with a light green trim.

Inside the house was a buffet line. The women who ran the establishment were older Olympia Food Co-op personnel. This was their new business venture.

One of them said hello to me. I got anxious about leaving my bike out front, so stepped out of line to go lock it. Before I could leave I was handed a teacup, white and elegant, full of soup. I walked down a couple of stairs, noticing the carpet was a pleasing light green color and there was a fireplace and living room below. The sliding glass door revealed a beautiful little lawn space with white iron lawn furniture.

I was in Santa Cruz with a bunch of young men, some of whom reminded me of boys I hung out with when I was a teenager. They had black t-shirts and were mostly poorly behaved.

I got a call on my cell phone as I stood next to the pool. As the men circled the pool talking and laughing I wondered if I had packed my swimsuit.

The phone call was from T. She jumped right in, talking in her excited voice, and asked me if I knew what I would be doing on a certain weekend (April 30th). She asked me in a way that seemed to suggest she already had a plan for me. She told me she was celebrating her birthday that weekend and wanted very much for me to be there.

I listened, amused and also touched, because she sounded like she was interested in talking to me, reconnecting, and willing to put energy into a new relationship with me.

All the while I considered what to wear to go swimming.

Finally, I asked her if I could call her back because I was traveling. She agreed.

Later, K. was in charge of driving us down the mountain. The longer she drove, the more weirdly slow and dangerous her driving. After the car went down the side of a short cliff, I said, with extra calm in my voice, *Do you want me to drive?*

I was actually very scared, having seen the nose of the car dip into nothingness. She said yes.

On the side of the road in the dust, we switched positions. I became the driver.

I wanted to buy a camera somewhere in Paris. Something was happening in the sky.

Ten moons in a pattern like a rainbow, curved, each moon in a different phase of moon-ness, unphotographable, laced the darkness. N. and I laughed, crying and gleeful at the spectacle: fish, fire, deer leapt from one moon onto the next until the jumble of colorful fauna finally jumped onto the last moon, extinguishing it.

Elton John was behind me at an outdoor pub, being ill. I did not want to turn to look.

I could not get the door to close in the apartment I'd recently moved into. K. happened by and saw me struggling in my pink silky robe that had fallen open, revealing my nakedness. A woman across the hall watched me try to fit the door into the frame. My robe continually fell open as I worked. The woman moved to help me, until we realized the door was just too small for the doorway. She then offered me a plate. On the plate lay a pair of green and yellow striped gloves, fried.

Later, in the large concrete library with one glass wall, the shaking began. The building turned completely on its side. I wanted to stop in a doorway but none seemed safe as we ran.

The earthquake ended. No one had been harmed.

MAY

I found a rabbit.

The rabbit belonged to the owner of the house who was hosting the party. I tried to capture it to put into a room because I feared it running loose around the many-storied house with so many strangers.

The rabbit had a one to two-foot-long elongated neck. I tried to not get sidetracked by that.

Wandering the house, I came across a photo in a black and white tabloid that showed many people, famous people. They too had elongated necks, like the rabbit's.

Michael sat in a tub of water with all of his clothes on.

On my way to school in Portland, I saw my professor, Michael Moore, at a bus stop.

When I showed up late for the test, he came over to my desk and showed me the many-paged exam with lots of his pen marks on it. He told me I was late and he didn't know if I could finish the test. I looked up at him.

"I know I'm late," I said. "They surrounded the bus stop I always leave from with orange cones and the bus was late, making my trip to school two hours long."

He put the exam on my desk.

I carried a large backpack, the one I take traveling, and in it was my light blue uniform from Catholic school. I had to change into it and did, covertly, for Michael Moore's class.

Also in my backpack was a bomb. It looked like a car battery, only instead of a digital readout showing the countdown, it resembled an old fashioned gas station readout: numbers that rolled into the next number.

I had about 4 minutes to place the bomb somewhere it could safely detonate and not hurt anyone.

I wasted 90 seconds trying to figure out where to take it. I jumped into a non-motorized vehicle and drove off under the cloudy sky.

When I found an elementary school set back in the woods, I knew I'd found the right spot. I walked right through the empty classrooms to the backyard, past the playground, where I spotted a deep marsh. It would be best to leave the bomb there. It could create a sinkhole and I might avoid taking any lives.

I left it in the marsh and mud and walked quickly back through the classrooms. The classrooms now had teachers in them, who eyed me as I moved to exit.

I knocked over someone's glass of iced tea. *Sorry*, I said, and left the building.

I didn't realize I had a serious cut in the bottom of my foot until I walked down the carpeted stairs of the unfamiliar house. I left a trail of thick blood in my wake.

I sat down in a chair and looked at the bottom of my foot. In the most tender part was a gash, and the blood wouldn't stop flowing.

Sharon Olds helped me clean up the cut. Her manner was gentle, mothering. I grimaced and squealed in her hands with the feel of the liquid she used stinging my open wound.

When I entered the room, kittens and rabbits were underfoot. Their soft fur brushed my feet and calves.

When the people in the room held me under my armpits and lifted my body up and down, in a dunking fashion, there was no pain.

My husband was convinced—and trying to convince me—that our adolescent son was Jesus Christ.

My husband was stocky and blond and didn't seem delusional, though I wondered.

My son was lean, tall, had blond hair and was clearly popular. His father did not want him listening to music, though it was apparent our son had a proclivity toward music—making it, and listening to it.

I watched my son surrounded by his friends, and yes, he gave off a nice aura, but was he Jesus?

My husband tried to keep music away from our son and I finally confronted him, pleasantly, on Hollywood Blvd. near Highland. I tried to reason with him. *Okay, you think our son is Jesus?* Yes, he replied. *Then that means I'm the mother of Jesus and I'm a virgin? And I can't have sex? No, I cannot accept that.* And left it at that

The drive to Olympia took 24 hours.

I stood in the aisle of the store where Michael worked and said, *Hi, I drove the 24 hours so I could just come say hi.*

I remembered I had to work the next day. Obviously there was not enough time to drive all the way back to Los Angeles. Why had I done this to myself?

Low-grade panic set in.

I made excuses to myself in my head. A 24-hour drive home loomed.

At the new dry cleaners, customers were required to write down emergency contact info.

For being a regular customer, the cleaners gave customers a stack of interesting brochures. One brochure was titled *OUTLAW PLANET* but when I looked again, it actually read *OUTLAW STREET*.

Michael was with me, so I asked him what his cell phone number was. He would be my emergency contact. He told me: *1-800-TREE-2*.

A piece of glass had lodged under the skin near my right hipbone after I fell. Though there was no torn skin, I could feel the hard nub of glass under the surface. I couldn't stop touching it with my finger.

Someone was supposed to help me remove it, but no one ever did.

JUNE

My elaborate outfit was composed of several red shawls and skirts overlapping one another into a loose dress.

I walked up and down a cement sidewalk in a park—Abigail and other friends on one end, the view of the city at the other end. The red of my dress was rich and beautiful.

Abigail had loaned me $5 and wanted it back right away. I showed her my wallet, the lone dollar bill crumpled in it.

I walked back toward the view of the city, as far away from her and the others as possible.

My charges were one large adult cat and two very tiny kittens.

Sarah, Andy, and I were on a road trip to a vacation. I expected a shoreline, a pier.

After we rented the black motorcycle we realized three people and three cats were not going to fit.

I chased the cats, calling their names, gathering them to me. The kittens in particular moved very fast in their tiny bodies.

The bar in the woods featured wood floors, high ceilings, party lights, and four poles.

The man who owned one of the poles told me that people rented the space for parties, and whenever a stripper used his pole to dance, he got a cut of the money.

He received a page on his pager. I could tell he was pissed. Many dances had happened and the numbers didn't add up, he explained. He felt ripped off.

I couldn't understand who kept track and who paged him.

S. and I made out, naked, in the top bunk of a bed in my childhood bedroom.

When he sat up on his knees and smiled down on me, I made him get back under the covers, quick. *My mom has a very bad habit of knocking on doors and then coming in without waiting for you to respond*, I said.

A moment later, my mother did just that, and I was thankful we were under the covers.

Mr. Connell conducted an essay test on the subject of how we've evolved and will evolve spiritually.

He handed me a hardbound book, which I understood to be my journal. I thought that was very clever, to hand us back our own journals to write on such a topic.

After writing a few pages I whispered back and forth with Abigail and lost my train of thought. She turned her book in. I scrambled to finish up, and wrote very small at the bottom of the fourth lined page. When I turned in my book to Mr. Connell, I was free to wander the unfamiliar house we were in.

I went in search of a bathroom. Both were unclean enough that I couldn't use them.

S. placed a framed photo of a woman on the windowsill above the sink.

I was intensely jealous of her. In the photo she was turning to look at the photographer, and her blond hair, nearly shaved, glinted in the sun.

He didn't take down the photo.

Michael and I went for a walk. As we walked around one side of the house, it became the sidewalk next to my mother's house.

Michael told me he had a bad knee. I asked why. "I followed a dog home last night," he said.

In the run-down hotel bar in the middle of the desert, I received a text message.

I had missed my dinner engagement with AQ.

Only fifteen minutes late, I messaged her back to tell her if she'd wait for me, I'd be there soon. Her reply was a mean-spirited message to the effect of "Fuck off." I was shocked and disappointed.

At the end of the play, in which I'd been the main character, I had to admit I had had an affair with a married man.

S. was in the audience. I hurriedly whispered in his ear that it was just a play and no such thing had really occurred.

My friends and I walked the cement paths next to lawns at the housing project. It was sunny.

Don't look that way, they told me, meaning, don't look at that big picture window we were passing. Sh. was inside, with a woman. They were filming each other. They lived there together.

I didn't look.

The couple S. and I were dining with in New York owned the place—a very luxurious and dark home.

The woman had short, straight brown hair and wore red lipstick. The couple appeared to be in their 40s, white and well-off.

There was something unusual about eating there.

When everyone got up from the table to go "sight-seeing," I pointedly remarked to S. that I wasn't ready to go. *Can't anyone see that?* I said, as I held the gingerbread, or cornbread, in my hands. Their plates were clean.

I could tell I had done something akin to a tantrum. Everyone settled back down to the table uneasily.

I was instantly angered. I barely knew these people, S. seemed to side with them, and I wasn't even having a good time.

S. and I were going to buy a new car. Lots of women in bright pink bikinis milled around the car lot. S. practically hurt his neck twisting and turning to eye the parade.

I sat in the backseat of the car as we drove off the lot, angry and silent.

JULY

There was something about the light of the moon.

As the *something* was happening, I realized it was just like the essay in which Annie Dillard writes about the total eclipse she witnessed.

The people around me were just as unsure as I was. We looked at the sky with a profound shared feeling of dread mixed with excitement. I knew it was the moon, it had to do with its light, but that was all I understood—that, and that huge sweeping changes would arrive in mere minutes, and no one was prepared.

The colors changed. Everything took on an otherworldly gloss. I felt myself grinning involuntarily because the rush of not knowing, of dread, of being thrilled to my marrow, was so strong.

Two unfamiliar men began chasing me. Finally, one of them, a tall blond, made peace with me. I still did not trust him. I could tell they were untrustworthy, especially together.

S. put his arm around me. I could feel his height, recognize his arm atop my shoulders. It was comforting to be near him again. The weight of him drew me closer.

I held a cooked rabbit with my fingers in an attempt to stuff it. I pulled the skin up, dipped my fingers into the bowls of nuts and stuffing. A bowl of broth stood by.

I lived with Michael in a strange house that we shared with Forbes. I couldn't believe we were in this situation. The house was noisy and dirty. Forbes and his friends had taken over the living room and some of the back bedrooms.

I stood in the kitchen with a washing machine that did not run on electricity. I looked inside its basin at a lot of cold water, bubbly with soap.

I went to my father's bedroom, where he lay in bed. A large lump of blankets waited on the floor next to the bed. I was curious about who was under there.

It was Sh. When I got over my shock, I listened as he told me he was working in Lake Tahoe. He and my father exchanged some comments about that. I wasn't even curious about what he was doing there or how he knew my father; I wanted to get him alone.

When we were alone, he told me he wanted to be with me again. My hesitance was a small mosquito trying to alight in my ear. I thought up questions I wanted to ask him, to sort of buffer any kind of hurt I might experience.

Question one: *Will I have to be monogamous again?*

I only thought this question to myself, never asking aloud. I mostly watched him talk, thoroughly delighted at his attentions and completely enchanted by his beauty, something we exchanged comments on in the first two days of knowing each other—glowing exchanges of how beautiful we found the other. I had never told a man before how beautiful I found him physically.

As I was thinking of questions, my heart sank. I knew that I would choose Sh. and where would that leave S.? I wondered how S. would react. It made me a little sick thinking of it but I looked again into Sh.'s face and all the doubts washed away, the mosquito found another ear to alight in, before the sinking feeling again.

I was with two of the younger boys from my adopted family. They were still little boys, while I was a young woman.

Their father was drove us around in a Vanagon. We stopped at a Taco Bell that had a bar inside. I ordered a Corona for $8.88.

We sat at a table, but everyone was restless. Finally, their father drove us to a park. It looked empty except for the other van we pulled up to, nose to nose, so close I could see the woman in the driver's seat of that van inch back in her seat like we were about to crush her. The woman turned out to be a friend of the boys. He took some flowers to the woman and stepped into her van. The boys and I went for a walk.

A while later, I decided to go back to the van and the boys followed. I lay down in the grass next to the parking space and closed my eyes. The van began to squeak a gentle rocking rhythm. I knew exactly what was happening and could hardly believe it. The boys' father had a lover. She was a long-haired brunette, an older hippie woman wearing tattered clothing. I thought about this, and his wife, and wondered if she had had lovers over the years too.

The boys seemed not to notice the squeaking and rocking. Soon after, their father stepped out of the other van and we got up to go. I heard the woman speak; she had a French accent.

AUGUST

After finding parking, then believing I should turn around and park elsewhere as Abigail suggested, I lost my parking space on the narrow incline with parallel parking spots. It was snowing.

When we finally had a place to park, there was a tall ladder to climb. It was not a normal ladder, but more like an industrial ladder, and the very last rung was abnormally high, so high that I had to have someone help me lift my leg high enough to reach it. I couldn't let up my pace because of the line of people behind me.

When I got to the top there was a little wooded area. The snow had been coming down slushy, but here, the amusement park was covered in thick snow. N. came over and put her arm around me as we talked to people we met up with there. The little white lights illuminating the park shut off, revealing a beautiful stillness in the cold night.

A pair of athletes moved to town. I watched them on television. It was unclear whether they'd be enrolled in college classes or just sitting in. The television told me they attended prayer meetings.

The day after I found out they were in town, I walked outside my apartment door. Crayon graffiti was smattered all over the door and doorframe of my apartment. The hallway was too dark to decipher what was written, but I was disturbed.

Later, I figured out the graffiti had to do with the two athletes.

I came across them, tried to question them, but they were evasive. One started to engage with me and eventually an attraction sparked.

We danced. It felt foolish, dancing in the street among strangers. He dipped and spun me. He used a makeshift lasso to playfully wrap and unwrap my legs.

My father's bedroom was filled with women. Women from my past, women I didn't know, everyone partying and laughing and bouncing and talking loudly.

I wandered through, looking at black and white photographs on the walls.

The photographs were candid shots of me and people I knew: one of my ex-supervisors, her son, S. Once or twice a photograph transformed into a short film: while I looked, the subjects moved, and a little scene played out.

My grandmother lay on the sofa in her sitting room. A black and yellow striped spider crawled on the floor and began climbing up the sofa arm. I expected it would crawl onto her if I didn't say anything... and I didn't say anything.

My mother hired a number of men to work on a garden at her house.

When I arrived, I observed the tools they were all using. The tools looked suspicious.

I understood the men were there to assassinate me.

I walked past, pretending to admire their work. I began to run down the street and the people I was with tried to block the men from reaching me. And they did.

Later, we holed up inside my mother's house. My mother was absent, possibly already dead. The people there to protect me coaxed me away from the windows where I might be seen. Their own fear was palpable even as it was bound up in a somber vigilance.

When I tried to call the police, it was clear the phones had been bugged.

I put the phone back into its receiver. If there was a secret closet or trapdoor in the house I didn't know about, my mother might be hiding out. This thought sustained me even as I could hear my assassins outside.

My mother never arrived.

SEPTEMBER

V. told me, *You are phenomenally beautiful.*

OCTOBER

The creature, part possum, part squirrel, stood on a picnic table smiling as my mother fed it with her hands.

In the house on the vast yellow plain I knew there was something to be scared of.

We stood outside with no cover as thick black storm clouds formed in the sky, moving at an impossible rate. We froze. Once they were positioned overhead, I knew this was something supernatural and, in fact, evil.

The downpour soaked us through. The clouds passed.

The scene repeated: black clouds. Downpour. An engulfing silence when they passed.

In the distance I saw an enormous train headed toward us. It came so fast that I could not tell which way to run—left, or right—and it was so huge there wasn't even enough time to run.

I ducked down on the ground and felt the train move over me. I had somehow placed myself right into the best, safest part of the tracks. The train passed into the distance and left us in the open mouth of silence once again.

The scene repeated. The second time I felt the metal on my back.

On the plain with not a single tree to ground us, we stood together crying and wringing our hands. I recited the 23rd Psalm, as my grandmother had taught me as a child. I recited over and over and over, tripping over some of the words, until she began to recite with me. We shouted it.

Another puncture would of black clouds formed and began heading toward us.

Summer, when the daylight stuck around until late. I had a road trip to make, Arizona to California. I would be driving across the desert alone all through the night.

I was nervous about this, but shared my fear with no one.

J. and I were on the yellow bedspread in the poorly lit motel room, having sex in as many positions as possible.

It had been awhile since I had to deal with condoms. The taste of one in my mouth reminded me.

Each sex act felt like a particular type of calisthenics, devoid of passion or affection. J. wanted to try a new position called "the afghan wig." It was actually something I'd never done—at least, it had never worked before.

Now it did.

Michael and I lived in a very nice one-bedroom apartment in a very old city.

Down the hall was another unit that my mother was cleaning, believing we might want to live in it.

I went to take a look. It was nice, but the windows were smaller and fewer. The covers on the bed were burgundy. I touched a sheet of plastic that encased them.

Michael would not like the colors (primarily burgundy), and I wanted the place with all the windows.

After my mother left, I wandered into the other rooms. In one was a piano with a candelabra on top, lit. Random pieces of lingerie spilled over the piano.

Instantly I knew the apartment had been vacated by Claire.

At the film festival in Olympia I sat on the cement outside the theater while lots of people milled around. With bright red paint I painted my leggings under my dress. The paint dripped from the thick paintbrush onto the hem. I painted over my thick socks and my shoes.

The cover of my little red book fell off.

My mother's house was haunted.

A tall woman with long braids repeatedly attempted to enter my father's old bedroom. A brown cat ran into the bedroom and the door closed behind it.

NOVEMBER

Abigail and I tread water in the middle of the ocean with almost no effort. A movie played, and I was entranced. The movie was about Jeff.

Someone had made a film about Jeff's life. One of the stars was the person who played Francis in *Malcolm in the Middle*.

The movie ended with a scene of Jeff being raped by Darth Vader. I was confused and disturbed. They killed one another with laser guns right before the credits rolled. I tried to understand what the symbolism might mean.

When the credits finished, I looked around and realized again we were in the middle of the ocean. The slow pump of adrenaline began. As soon as we began to swim, we glided, glided so fast we reached the shore within minutes.

We talked about the film the whole time.

At sewing class, everyone had a green cloth binder. I was the new student and would be receiving mine shortly.

I did not know how to start or what I would make. I glanced at other desks and saw little satin pillows that another student had made.

I waited patiently for my cloth binder.

I hiked a very steep incline into the snow.

It was sunny, clear and perfectly warm at the low-budget beach resort. K. was getting married to a woman who looked like a young Gertrude Stein.

The young Gertrude Stein never spoke. K. told me Anya was due to arrive at 8 a.m. that day, the morning of the wedding. The wedding would take place at 5 p.m. I thought 5 p.m. seemed kind of silly, but it meant that I could spend all if not most of the day in the water.

By 8:30 a.m. Anya still hadn't arrived. I used the excuse of going to find her to get down from the cliff we were on to the water. Though the wedding was the most important event of the day, and I wanted to be present for K., I felt the strongest urge to abandon it all to go be in the ocean.

DECEMBER

I stood with Kate Gale outside in the wide-open space. The fence's enormous gate was open.

Our conversation was amicable.

Nine bear cubs appeared from afar. Having seen us, they ambled in our direction, faster and faster. I yelled and Kate turned to look. She hurriedly ran to the gate to shut it, just in time.

Sh. surprised me when he arrived to my birthday party on Kingsley. When he left after a little while I pretended not to notice.

I was busy taking photos of little plastic Ken dolls on my Formica table. The dolls were in all kinds of sexual positions. As I was about to shoot, the door opened and Sh. was back. He held a box with a fake flower on it.

I told him he didn't have to, and opened the box. Inside were proof sheets and random negatives.

Every photo was of me.

I looked through them all. I realized he was essentially giving me back every scrap of evidence he ever had of me, of our relationship.

JANUARY

We were ordered to get on a plane to Poland.

There was no tarmac; we descended an impossibly long ladder underground.

I was a little nervous, but made my way down hundreds of feet just fine.

FEBRUARY

I watched one of my cats give birth to kittens, nine of them.

I approached my car and saw that all the tires were flat.

I hiked in a beautiful golden place. I saw a waterfall, and became instantly enchanted.

A group of us stood at the thrift store counter by the park. I waited for someone to finish talking so I could ask the clerk a question.

As I waited, a group of people of various ages came in and threatened everyone in the thrift store. When they turned to leave, the group I was with made a run for it. I led them to the park, knowing that something would have to change fast in the situation because the park was small and surrounded by a brick wall.

The threatening group had no trouble finding us. I wanted nothing more than to stop and figure out how I knew this park. There were plastic displays that looked like UFOs, which, when taken in context, led me to think the park was dedicated to UFOs. The leader of the threatening group made us stand in a line with our backs against the wall. A woman from their group told us they were looking for a message.

I pulled down my jacket, unveiling the tattoo on my arm. *This is a message,* I said in a growl.

I could tell they were impressed. I told them it was Latin. I did not reveal the translation. I knew that leading them in this direction—making them think we were a key to something, and therefore could not harm us—would work.

I was over 12 weeks pregnant.

I had become pregnant via saliva or some other liquid. However it happened, it seemed too simple.

My belly protruded and I looked at in the mirror. My heart sunk. I did not want to be pregnant.

I kept counting and recounting the months until when the baby would arrive. When I thought of the pain involved, a depression folded me up inside its jaws.

I was unprepared for this kind of change, this kind of pain.

T. invited me to her wedding. I was shocked. I brought fruit as an offering.

The room where the reception was held was quite small and looked full already with only seven people in it.

One man ate from a bowl decorated with multiple carvings of bulls. On another plate were bright blue and green rosebuds, no stems, made completely of sugar.

MARCH

My father planned to commit suicide.

When I found out, I was in my mother's house. Huge wracking sobs came out of my body. It wasn't until I saw my half-brother, and he gave me an indication that it wasn't going to happen, that I calmed down.

Outside, on a field, cheerleaders stood in rows or performed, all different outfits, various states of undress. S. and I settled down to watch. His grin, the way he put his chin in his hands as he lay on the ground to enjoy the show, was a little too much for me.

It was my second night ever stripping. The time before had not been a pleasant experience.

The venue was in Anaheim, so it was a long drive. When I got there I immediately knew I would probably not do more than one dance.

Everyone was coupled up in the large dark room. There were het and homo couples, and everyone was in the midst of some sex act. It was not an orgy; it looked like a class. There were so many different people of all different looks, sizes, colors and combinations. My job was to dance up and down the aisles for them.

At the tail end of the party someone insisted we eat the huge rectangular slab of tofu left on the table. The top half had been eaten off.

When we lifted it out of the container an army of cockroaches scurried out. I told everyone to stop eating it.

In the open-air bar, we all tried to remember the last few lines to the song "Sittin' on the Dock of the Bay" by Otis Redding. I plugged my ears and tried singing it to myself to see if I could remember but drew a blank every time. The whole bar, filled with people from my past and present, was in on the task. No one could think of how to finish the song.

I was at my mother's house, lying on a bed in my old bedroom. Jesse was visiting. I knew it was strange that he was visiting me, but my plan was to flirt and get information out of him before he left.

I knew my mother would find it strange that this man was in my room, and it was very late. I took my chances.

He lay across the bed with me. I smiled and lowered my eyes at him and coquettishly asked if he knew whatever happened to Jeff. He chuckled to himself. He said Jeff had become a Muslim and started his own mosque.

I was astounded by the information but hid it.

We laughed together about how excited Jeff could become over things, how enflamed he could be. I pushed for more information and Ed hinted that Jeff had married someone much younger than him.

How young? I asked.

Oh, eight to nine years younger, he said.

That's not that much younger! I said.

When my mother came into the room I realized that would be the end of the conversation. She pulled me aside and asked me who Jesse was and what he was doing there.

I said he was an old friend. I kept calm and told her he would be leaving soon.

I watched a previously unreleased version of *The Exorcist*. Colonies of small dark animals ran around, flying in patterns.

I beat S. over the head with a wooden spoon until he fell semi-conscious to the floor. I found out he was cheating on me. He showed no remorse.

I had a long conversation with T., which was pleasant and light and made me look forward to future conversations.

.

APRIL

My hair was being braided. The stranger doing it pulled my hair back from my scalp with a brush.

As they braided I could feel their hands moving in the motion of braiding.

In the bathroom there was a claw foot tub. A pink and orange yarn rug lay on the tile.

Two small balls rolled across the floor. I picked one up.

The ball was the size of a marble and covered in glitter. I put it in my mouth.

After I got over the taste of the glitter, and the worry that the glitter would somehow harm me, I chewed and chewed. It was like chewing a Jujube—gummy, sticky, too sweet.

MAY

The woman with three legs wore a pastel business suit. She pulled up to the sidewalk in a golf cart. The golf cart had a stick shift and the stick itself was shaped like a beautiful burgundy metal handbag. The woman didn't seem fazed by her third leg, which loped along in the middle of her other two legs. She could even make it dance by itself while the other two legs were unmoving.

I was deeply involved with both Ren and S. I had to leave one to return home to the other. Ren's friends told me that he was over at the Valencia movie theater where he had organized a movie-going night where activists went twice a week, so I went home to S.

Sitting across a long table while he read the newspaper, I said I had something important to tell him. He listened as I told him that I had been having a relationship with Ren, but I wanted him, S., more, and would end the other relationship.

S. was only slightly troubled by this admission.

I drove back and forth up and down a long hill that led me to and from the beach. On these trips, I mentored a young goth.

I met with her and made appointments to look at her writing once a week though I was never sure if I would see her again. She was hard to reach.

Each time I drove up and down the long curvy hill, I wished I could just stay down at the beach.

It was night and we were lakeside. S. and I were one of many couples. Later, when I tried to write down what I remembered for the police, I wrote "Katie and Paulo" though I faltered when writing Paulo's name because I knew they were no longer a couple, and then I wasn't sure what I remembered.

We all waded into the lake, which was warm. Each couple was making out in the water, no one really paying attention to other couples. My feet bounced along the lake bottom. I was happy, excited by the energy.

Moments later, when my feet bounced against something that was not the lake bottom, I paused. I did not let on that anything was wrong. I could hear laughter. Everyone was enjoying themselves.

When I bounced again, I knew what my feet were hitting. I was hitting the wrists and arms of a human body.

When I walked out of the lake, I carried Hope in my arms. She was dead. Everyone who had been in the water was now on shore. Some cried and shrieked. My chest heaved with the effort of both carrying Hope's body and sobbing. I carried her to the sand and lay her down.

We stayed with her through the night and into morning. Men in suits came to visit but I understood they were her friends. By then she was in a body bag wearing a shimmery white dress. Her eyes were closed. When I looked at her once, I saw her eyes open and she was breathing. I cried out and looked away.

A man in a suit told me that he had opened the body bag and she had heaved a great sigh and then vomited. I was afraid to look back at her.

My father arrived. In the midst of crying and all the people milling around, I had to explain who Hope was.

One of my cousins drove my car away. I was left with my mother, who was raging drunk.

I knocked her down and she bloomed upright.

I punched her again.

She fell, then levitated back up into a standing position. My mother was a punching clown, unable to stay down.

As I continued beating her up—and she continued to stand upright—I decided to call the police and report my car stolen.

S. and I agreed to marry in May, almost two years before we thought we might.

We planned, in a matter of minutes, a wedding in San Francisco.

Our procession took place on very long, winding asphalt path that looked like a runner's course. Hundreds of people stood at the end of the path. I wore a long dress with a light brown and tan print that flounced out at the bottom. When we reached our audience, I knew I needed the blue bra.

In front of all the guests I managed to discreetly change bras.

Eventually we went back to where the procession began. Everything took much too long and I was fearful of my mother's reaction. I looked in a mirror and one side of my face was hairy. I would have to shave it. In the dressing room, populated by dancers, I quietly picked up someone's razor and quickly removed the hair from my face. I felt the eyes of the dancers on me from behind a curtain.

I returned to S. and readied to make the long walk. I reiterated to him that my father would not have to accompany me, that I found that practice creepy. Elsa, who was in charge of the events, rushed down and asked, "What is taking so long?" The wedding was to start at 10 a.m. It was already after 11. The procession started once again.

S. and I walked at different paces. He walked several paces away and asked if he could play "The Ocean" though I knew he meant "Across the Universe" by the Beatles. We rounded the corner where all the people wait-ed, in bleachers covered in white.

I went inside and watched all the people leaving, the place emptying out. It was dark outside. Snowflakes began to fall.

My mother's head was in a puddle of water and I put a pillow over her face.

At the very last moment before she could drown or suffocate, I removed the pillow. I was overcome with sorrow and pain at my actions.

I put the pillow back over her face.

JUNE

I packed and repacked my bags. I left them in a room to go outside.

A silver shimmer moved through the outdoor fountain. A huge swordfish pushed through the water and hit air. Panic set in—the swordfish was the size of a small truck. I wanted to look but also wanted to run. I knew that many things would suddenly be growing huge in size. I wasn't sure where to go.

I went back inside to find my bag. Gone. I searched the room. Inside the closets lay piles of my clothes, but I wanted the clothes in the black bag.

As I headed back out to figure out what my next move would be, AQ came by. She told me she was leaving with someone, a man I didn't know. She asked if she could borrow my bike. Everyone was afraid to drive their cars, so I said yes, she could leave on my bike. I watched her walk away with my pink bike. I knew she was frightened.

I wasn't entirely sure how I would get out of that place. More gargantuan swordfish leapt through the fountain.

I walked up and down and around the path to the ocean. The path wound around tidepools. One in particular was dark and frothy. I was afraid to jump in.

Abigail jumped in.

She accompanied me on all these trips back and forth to the ocean, past the whirlpools and other people, even in the dark. We had no sense of time; there was just the walking back and forth in this mysterious and beautiful place, knowing the beach was within walking distance.

I tried explaining to S. that Abigail had jumped into the whirlpool but that I could not. I pointed at it and it still seemed too menacing, as though it could suck you up and spit you out. Abigail had come out okay, but I was still wary of it. My black swimsuit was slick and shiny, even more shiny when wet.

I was a young prostitute, about 15, with straight dirty-blond hair. I lived in a large, dark room with blue walls with several other women of all ages and looks. Most of the women were dressed in paisley or jeans or hippie blouses. One woman dressed like a 90s Olympia riot grrrl. She was the one sent out every day and night while the rest of us stayed in.

When I got out to the red-walled restaurant, I noticed that all of her clients were young women like herself. Everyone wanted her. She never spoke and I barely ever saw her because her time was too precious and was spent with all of her clients. I almost forgot she was one of us and lived with us.

The best part about her being "out there" all the time was that the rest of us were not pressured to go out. I lied in bed a lot in the large blue room with my bank of light switches next to me.

The man in charge of us was white, tall, thin, attractive. He wore a 1960s-era light blue suit. He had blue eyes and was very kind. I was used to his kindness.

When, one night, no one could locate the woman that was always out working, and there began rumors that she didn't even live among us anymore, and that she never really had, the man in charge became angry. I tried to switch off all the lights from my bed before he could find me. I wore my light blue silky nightgown and hid as much as I could hide on the perch of my dark bed.

Dread filled the room when he found me. I tried to convince him she was still one of us and would return. He was no longer kind.

He grimly told me that we would *all* be going out every night, every one of us.

I was filled with despair thinking of us all being forced to go out and work in the night now. I was filled with despair that he had lost his kindness completely.

JULY

I drank an entire green bottle's worth of water. The water was milky-colored. It belonged to my boss.

I shaved my legs for hours, with utmost intensity.

I was the new stripper in the club, earnestly learning the ropes. I had a hard time with one satiny red costume.

I went on a date with Jerry Seinfeld, whom I discovered I liked very much.

JULY

Sandy and I went out to lunch. She urged me to choose between her and S.

I wouldn't.

I was on the verge of tears because some part of me knew that I was deeply conflicted and there was no way out.

AUGUST

S. was one of my two boyfriends.

I was fairly certain S. would not like finding out about my other boyfriend so I kept them separate.

I never allowed the other boyfriend to sleep over at my house, which I shared with S. The whole situation was a done deal and it had been going on this way for a while, so there was nothing to be done.

Standing on a corner, surrounded by tall buildings and a park, everything stopped.

The stillness took on a sound. That sound grew louder and louder.

Oh my god, I said. I hoped there wouldn't be an earth-quake.

As soon as I had the thought, the ground shook violently.

I ran through the streets with other strangers, trying to look up and down to make sure buildings wouldn't topple over on us, trying to make the sure the ground we were about to dash across wouldn't open up under our feet.

In two different houses, each living room was given over to a certain type of art project. The second house was white with cactus out front. I went in.

The house belonged to Morgan. The living room was set up very strategically. A number of young men worked on computers or did other tasks in one of the other rooms.

The art project centered around entering the room, looking around, opening drawers, finding clues. A mystery had occurred there. I gathered clues.

The blue carpet was marked with black arrows. A ceiling fan twirled. The desk drawers hung open.

I was very impressed by this project.

SEPTEMBER

AQ's house was hidden behind a grove of trees with thick, knotty trunks and long, lithe branches and foliage that covered the skyline. It made the front yard very dark. An Isuzu Trooper was parked underneath the trees.

Two large windows were wide open with only curtains blowing in the wind. I climbed in one of the windows.

It was strange that AQ had left the windows open. I looked around the house for signs of anything missing, though I couldn't really tell since I didn't know what had been there in the first place.

The man who accompanied me was tall and wore a sharp black suit. He had dark brown hair and appeared very professional, even suave. We'd happened upon something unusual I couldn't put my finger on. There was no way to close the windows and this concerned me.

Vampires entered the house through the windows.

We managed to fend them off. I ran to the front window. A man and a woman got into the Trooper and drove away. *Do they know AQ?* I thought.

I ran back to the other side of the house to help the man decide what we would do, how we would secure the house from anyone else entering. Possibly, but especially, vampires.

OCTOBER

I walked down the hallway looking inside classrooms. I looked for Room 7. None of them were labeled.

I peeked inside one room that said "Composition 1" on the board. The tables and chairs were suitable only for preschooler-sized bodies.

NOVEMBER

I had a son—a stepson—in his 20s. He looked a little like Jude Law. His father was largely absent.

We were quite wealthy and in the Latin American town we lived in, our family had financed the bus service, so when we got on the bus, a townsperson came up to me and lavished me with thanks, taking my arm, stroking and patting it.

My (step)son and I had a strange relationship. We were very attracted to one another and walked around with an arm around each other's waists. I heard someone mention the queer way we held one another, that it didn't look "motherly." It looked like something else. We mostly kept ourselves in check but often we looked at each other and said things to each other that made our attraction known to ourselves. We also tried to keep it under constraint, and no move was made to consummate anything. Seeing him laid out, nude, I wanted to touch him—the light blond hairs on his chest and belly—but I managed to just look and smile.

A boat went by in the canal and my stepson wondered aloud if they had stolen his idea. He'd started a mode of transportation that had gambling on board. It indeed looked like someone else had started that on a boat.

We went back to our walk, me pausing to circle my arms around his waist, clasping my hands together to hold him.

DECEMBER

I was in a pizza restaurant and a young boy was behind the counter. I had a handful of frozen peas. I pushed one pea down a little toy chute that sat on the counter. I paid with a handful of pennies.

S. and I lived in an apartment with a view of a large grassy field. Beyond it was a freeway interchange with heavy traffic.

I was out in the field alone. I wore my running clothes because I'd been exercising. I relaxed, lay on the grass, stretched, looked at the sky and back at the apartment. A loud crack forced me to look in the direction of the freeway, where plumes of black smoke rose. The final crack that sent me running ended in a long, eerie metallic sound, louder than anything I'd ever heard before.

I ran back toward our apartment as the black smoke filled the sky. S. was inside but the door was locked. I pulled on the knob frantically before he unlocked it. People from our building ran out their doors, jumped in cars, fleeing.

S. began to melt down. In the midst of his crying and stammering, I asked him if he thought we should try to leave.

"No," he said, his voice quavering "We can't because of the cats."

I saw his point.

My mother, father and I went to Venice Beach. We stayed in a small room with one bed that we shared with a group of young mothers and their young children.

My parents went out ahead of me—either to the bar or to go swimming—and I stayed behind. Not only was my bathing suit becoming a nuisance, but I was suddenly extremely hairy.

I was in Joshua Tree but not.

In order to get to the beautiful place across the way, I had to cross a super-long, skinny, swinging bridge. I did it with no problem. Later I wanted to return to the same place, so I began crossing again.

What's wrong? I asked Veronica after seeing some people leaning over the bridge, ill.

It occurred to me I didn't need to cross that bridge again. I had already been across once.

I watched someone get into a car driven by John Lennon. Yoko Ono was in the passenger seat. Two small children were in the back.

Packing and repacking, in a hurry, my hair misbehaving. Was I going to be able to defend my thesis?

Running, I jumped on a moving subway train to get my clothes and gear.

JANUARY

S. and I were busily trying to have sex in my mother's side yard.

I was wet and writhing. From my vantage point, I saw the blinds in the bedroom window being opened.

My grandmother was spying on us.

I yelled at the top of my lungs: YOU ARE DISGUSTING AND I'M HORRIFIED YOU'D WATCH US.

"She is seriously sexually repressed," I told S., "and therefore perverse."

FEBRUARY

I had two dresses to choose from.

The first was a black-and-white print, long and flowing rayon. When I wore it, I looked impossibly thin.

The second came in two pieces. The top was green and the bottom brown. It was heavy, felt-like. In the mirror I appeared five times larger than normal.

We ended up by the ocean. The bus drove directly next to the see-through water. I watched people swim as though they were magnified, every detail visible.

Without warning, a shark fin appeared. It cut swiftly toward a tall, elderly couple. The bus took up a collective scream as we watched the shark bite the man and swim past, then come back around for more. *Get out of the water!* we shouted. Our cries could not be heard.

Helicopters vibrated in the sky. The man got out of the water. He had only minor wounds.

MARCH

When I woke up, I had to call Nicholas. I had left him in Joshua Tree the day before. Had I paid for an extra camp-site for us? Was he camping with his family?

S. clicked away at the keyboard and the stereo was on, loud. I stood up and got my cell phone to call Nicholas. I had trouble finding his number, then more trouble trying to dial. Nicholas finally answered. He'd guessed I wasn't going to be coming out again, since I had just left the day before.

"I'm becoming Bettyphobic," he said. He wasn't look-ing forward to talking to Betty. It was pointless to ask why because the stereo was too loud. I tried to turn it off but it was stuck, unable to switch off. Nicholas told me he was going fishing. I asked him where but couldn't hear his reply.

"This stereo's not turning off," I said to S. He shrugged and went back to what he was doing at his computer.

Nicholas sounded a long way off. I could barely hear him. At least he understood I was not returning that day.

The enormous "lucky 13" tattoo on my left forearm was exquisitely detailed. The black was rich, and there were subtle flames and careful shading that made it jump off my skin.

Still, I wasn't certain I wanted to have that on me for life.

MAY

I was on my way to where I knew Jeff would be. I caught a glimpse of him; I tried to get away from where I knew he would be arriving.

I entered the computer room. Everyone but Nicholas hugged me. He was late getting me a flyer, and it didn't look very professional.

I hugged the two women in the room. Another woman we knew of had been raped. *Stay safe*, we told each other. I told them I'd experienced the same at the hands of my teacher.

The large woman with long, straight, dishwater-blond hair expressed surprise. The second woman hugged me longer, wouldn't let go of me easily. I smiled and hugged her back with just as much energy as I felt from her.

Nicholas, I could see, was having more of a problem offering me a hug.

JUNE

Claire was in art school. Her focus was film and video. I wandered the halls, watched people at computers.

I had to catch my plane so I looked for a free computer and found one. I tried to log on to the website where I could print my boarding pass. Of course the page had problems loading.

It was 5:30 p.m. I didn't want to check my notes, waste more time. I figured I had already missed my flight.

JULY

I was a little girl. I ran from room to room, chased by two parents who looked like something from *Leave It to Beaver*.

Every time they caught me in a room, I screamed and cried and stamped my feet.

I took a chunk of eggplant in my hands. The skin came off beautifully, the entire body was like the texture of an orange with its peel off.

AUGUST

While his wife was in a dance class, I sat near the ocean with the man I had a crush on and his parents. As I watched the surf, a big black something twirled out of the water.

The sea turtle lumbered up on shore and sat in my lap. As I pet it, it became a seal.

I looked into its eyes. My crush sat behind me, holding the rest of the seal on his lap.

I was caught in a flood.

I delivered the baby by C-section and carried the infant in my arms. I walked up to a gas station. There were bloodstains on the concrete garage floor. Two people behind me saw the stains. I could hear their reaction. It appeared someone had been dragged across the floor, bleeding.

I decided not to look in the direction of the dead body and called the police.

The man scurrying around the gas station might have committed the murder. He asked me who I had called.

My baby was no longer in my arms.

The man threatened me with a large plastic spatula. I lunged at him and took it out of his hands. *I've just had a baby and I'm not afraid of anything*, I thought.

S. and I escaped to the lakeside resort I've often been to at night. Twenty cats populated the room with wood paneling. In the midst of all the cats was a woman with gray hair. She was one of the owners of the resort. A gaggle of babies were on the couch with not enough people to hold them. I took one into my arms and went back outside to the truck to find S. He sat in the driver's seat, reading and smoking.

SEPTEMBER

My right eyelid was swollen. I investigated it as best I could in the mirror.

I looked through a book of black pages. My adopted brother had copied out poems, drawn pictures and cut out images he'd pasted to the pages.

The poems had a theme of intersexuality. I mentioned this and asked who the author was. He told me a name I did not recognize. I skipped the pages where there were photos and drawings of me.

OCTOBER

I gave birth to a baby girl.

I was at my mother's house. I was dressed in a white half-slip and long-sleeved white silk shirt.

A cat asked me if I would nurse her.

I knew it was weird. I looked around. I could find a private place. I said yes.

In my childhood bedroom, I situated the cat on one breast and the little girl on the other. I called the little girl "Lupita."

S. and I played in the ocean. When the tide quickly headed out, impossibly fast, revealing the sand and shells and animals as it went further and further out, I knew we had to make a run for dry land.

We were among the few to survive when the tidal wave hit shore. From the concrete I watched the tide get sucked back out, taking all of our towels, wallets, belongings.

I pushed my hand into my pocket. There was my car key. It was all alone, and it was all we had, but it was something, and that was huge.

NOVEMBER

Sarah and I lived in the sixth-floor apartment.

I was in the stairwell, a little fearful that the doors might be locked and then I wouldn't be able to get out of the stairwell, but the door opened. I saw our floor.

Down the hall I heard Sarah talking. I walked the hallway with its orange walls and shocking orange and white striped carpets. I made my way toward her voice.

DECEMBER

The apartment owner came in and asked if I had the ladder. I told her yes, and led her into the apartment.

The ladder was thin and tangled up in our curtain. As I untangled it, I told her that I'd also put a note on the door of apartment #205. She smiled, which was rare, and we made small talk about the tenants as I freed the ladder.

I was on the long bus ride to Olympia. Before I made it there, I got off at the wrong stop a few times, walked in the rain, ran down a sidewalk too close to cars and had other adventures.

When I got to the restaurant I was relieved it was only 11:30 a.m. and figured that Michael would be awake by now, so after I ate, I could go to his house and visit him, which was my plan all along.

As I stood at the counter waiting to pay, I noticed two strange pieces of artwork on the walls, and a taped-up advertisement on each that noted the restaurant's inclusion in some books or films. The advertisements were written in black marker on a paper cut-out of an old-fashioned red hot dog.

As I looked at them, someone put their arm around my waist. It was Michael. I looked up at him and smiled and told him I was planning to surprise him.

It wasn't his arm around me, though—a moment later I realized it was our friend C., who happened to be staying with him.

I was in a large empty gray brick building on the corner of Woodman and Sherman Way. A lot of us were inside—we all lived there. A man and a group of contractors or laborers were also inside and we were told to stand still. The man in charge had a large steel wheel in his hands that he turned. As he maneuvered it, the entire building shifted until it had been moved 180 degrees from its original orientation. I was amazed—I had no idea buildings could be moved like this. Michael was talking excitedly to the contractor afterward, no doubt just as incredulous as I was. I noticed that everything was simply switched around now, including the little hot dog and popcorn cart on the first floor.

On the same block, I had a table and belongings set up on the sidewalk. I was typing on my laptop until it hit me that I should not be advertising the fact that I have a laptop right out on the street. Moments later a teenage boy and girl approached me and began reaching for my laptop and taunting me. I moved into a crowd of people at a bus stop, clutching my laptop. I tried calling for help, and fought with them as much as I could with my hands full. Finally, I got lost in the crowd and got onto a bus, relieved. I covered my laptop with my blue paisley shirt.

When I got off the bus, I saw familiar buildings. These buildings looked like something in an old country, though, that had long ago been conquered in a war and left to rot, but they were beautiful. The buildings had lofts, and were missing the entire building face, but flowers and trailing green leaves were growing from inside and continuing down to the ground. I walked by them to my house, where I lived with a man and a woman in a polyamorous relationship. I climbed over the new white furniture in the doorway. There were little signs on the furniture—clearly our female lover had left her mark, wanting us to enjoy the fruits of her labor. She was reminding us to enjoy the sensual and even the surreal. I had flashes of all the ups and downs I had with these two people. I was relieved to have my laptop and this sexy place to live. The two of them were in the next room so I put my stuff down and made a plan to return to the corner where I'd left the rest of my belongings.

JANUARY

Nicholas and I hung out at my mother's house. He asked if I'd finally asked S. if it would be a problem if I had sex with him before S. and I got married.

S. was not happy about it, but he said okay.

The party we went to was incredibly popular until someone got the idea to move it elsewhere and call it the same thing and charge $5. So the party began trickling through the gates to move elsewhere. I moved with it.

The sauna room was well-lit. I stood in line behind John and Veronica and a couple of others. A young blonde woman was facilitating the line and access to the sauna. Most odd was that she was also cleaning a cat box at the same time.

On the second level of the two-story house we stood and talked. From my conversation with the unknown man I understood that the house was ours and we were standing in only one half or one quarter of it. I could walk across a threshold and be in a completely identical other "half" of the house. He said that once someone took care of the boulevard behind the place to make it safer, we were set; this place would be perfect.

I peeked out back and knew what he was talking about—it was clear that someone had thrown bombs in at one time and I knew that the alley was used for drug deals.

We walked across to the other side of the place and I joked that we could each comfortably live in our own half of the place. The man went along with this idea for fun.

We entered a room with stereo equipment, masculine clothes strewn around, and the television was left on. DVDs and games were strewn around the tv.

I pressed eject and the DVD came out of a multiple disc holder. The title sounded like gay porn to me and I asked my companion about it—*Does so-and-so watch this? Is it kind of like porn?* Yes, he told me, it was a great show, actually, and I should see it.

We looked at the ocean through glass in the underground aquarium. Creatures swam, plants wafted in the movement of the tide.

A loud booming sound interrupted the undulating water fauna. In the next room over, the aquarium wall busted inward. It was a matter of time before the glass broke and all the water poured in, along with the creatures.

Nine women and I headed out to the ocean when darkness fell. As I stepped into the water, I had a sense of fear, but with all the other women I knew that somehow I'd be fine, even though I didn't have a clear sense where we'd be swimming to, or for how long. I wore a bathing cap I'd never seen before.

We swam in the twilight toward an ocean liner. We would be pulled up on board and this was just the practice run; the next night we'd have to swim toward it, get on it, and then they'd drop us off further out in the ocean, so we could swim with whales.

The idea both shook me and pleased me. I felt hot, flush.

I opened a carton of eggs. Every egg was broken.

I switched rooms in the unfamiliar, many-roomed house. We all had to share it, and everyone kept switching rooms.

In one bedroom, the blinds were drawn. There seemed to be the flicker of a candle upsetting the shadows. The large painting on the wall began to vibrate then shake violently. It was daylight when the shaking stopped. I jumped out of bed.

Through the window I saw two young boys coming up the walk. They were both very blond, blue-eyed, and looked to be about 12 and 14. When they entered the house, everyone was surprised and instantly happy to see them. I noticed that my boss and his wife seemed particularly glad and very warm toward these two. I began watching their interactions.

As I watched the boys, it occurred to me that they had appeared right after the violent shaking of the painting. Their appearance was somehow connected.

Looking at my boss and his wife, I realized that these boys were their children in some future-time. I was stunned. I tried to explain to someone else how bizarre this was. I wanted to make plain the 'logic' that if these were their future sons, what happened to them early on that they would appear now, not having grown up with their parents?

I was convinced inwardly that something traumatic had happened. They could not have appeared naturally as their sons, growing up with them.

I wanted to understand how they'd come into being.

The woman was American but told me she spent a lot of time in Germany.

She had short black hair and blue eyes and seemed a little older than me. We stood in the long hallway up above the music show, talking about environmentalism. She sounded hardcore.

I told her that while I've done plenty of environmentalist stuff in the past, the one thing I couldn't deal with was recycling shit. She asked me what I meant. I told her that I couldn't deal with it, just couldn't deal with shit and vomit. I tried to make a joke out of it. She was unimpressed.

When I walked away from her later, I remembered that Michael used to take all our old pizza boxes and refurbish them into cat scratchers, and wondered if that would impress her.

Later, while I talked to another woman, an Armenian woman and her mother approached. The young woman, maybe in her 30s, thanked us for our help. She had had the sponge removed—"All those hormones, ach!" She and her mother showed us the daughter's pregnant belly.

When they walked away I said to the woman with me, "There're hormones in the sponge? I had no idea."

I began looking at medical charts written on long pieces of graph paper. H. had written in some of them. I marveled at how her normally beautiful handwriting turned into that of a doctor's, the way it became illegible when written on medical charts.

FEBRUARY

Someone was doing a mathematics equation on the chalk-board.

The students and I watched the teacher write out equations and call out answers. Sometimes the answers had to do with our lives.

I said something about my life. About how it did not follow the equation to its conclusion.

I walked around an overlook where I could see Magic Mountain with an older man. He put his tongue in my mouth and I was disturbed. It felt like a little sliver of leather poking around my mouth.

Still, I let him hold me as we walked around the park in the dust. In the large public bathroom, I painstakingly cleaned up the toilet seat and flushed because the person before me had not.

I held hands with the giant. My guess is that he was over seven feet tall. When I looked up at him I had to throw my entire head back and bend my neck.

As I stroked his unbelievably huge cock, I asked, *What must it be like to take all of this in?*

"Anything smaller is just a sort of hello," he replied.

I was flabbergasted.

I was an Israeli spy.

Michael and I were getting married. He wore a very fancy black dress that he could rip off to reveal pants and shirt.

Drug deals went on outside the reception. No one knew when the wedding ceremony was to begin. I had to see S., though I didn't want to.

MARCH

I had to save the little girl.

I walked up to my car, in a hurry to get away from whoever was after us. All the windows had been smashed out. I hurriedly opened the back door and brushed as much glass as I could from the seat to lay the little girl on it safely. She was upset and crying most of the time, especially when I had to leave or when I was merely out of her eyesight. I tried to explain that we were in a hurry and it would all be okay soon. I ran around the other side of the truck, fumbling with my keys.

NOW

I walk through the tunnel and am aware of walking through it. As soon as I become aware, things shift.

Drinking a cold-brew coffee on a sidewalk in Santa Monica, Jerry says, "You're supposed to look at your hands before you sleep." I've heard that before. I haven't tried any of the lucid dreaming techniques I've read about it.

I walk through the tunnel and tell myself, *I am walking through the tunnel. Stay here. Stay here.*

On the picnic bench in our backyard, I tell Sandy, *I think I know the ending now.* It's a practice.

The walls of the tunnel morph into colors that spill around me. I temper my excitement at what is happening. What will happen.

You're here.

You're aware.

This is the beginning.

INDEX

ACKNOWLEDGEMENTS

Thank you, Michael J. Seidlinger, for everything you do.

For the task of indexing, a special award goes to Sandy Lee, who completely dedicated herself to this project: indexing on the sofa while I watched t.v., by the side of the road, occasionally asking me things like, "Do you agree that 'manhole' is a word that should be indexed?" and making statements like, "I'm just gonna finish cataloging the entry of 'mother' since it's so extensive" . . . I could not ask for a more incredible partner.

Thanks to my oldest friends irl & on that other plane: Sarah Buller, Melanie Klein, Katie Rose Alexander, and Andrea Saenz.

Special thanks to Dodie Bellamy, Scott Cheshire, Elizabeth Crane, Adrienne Crezo, and Roxane Gay. Your generosity means so much to me.

Deep appreciation to Meredith Alling, Lauren Eggert-Crowe, Rae Gouirand, Arielle Greenberg, Myriam Gurba, Karrie Higgins, Chelsea Hodson, Brian Kornell, Sarah Pape, Jennifer Pashley, Jerry Pyle, Ruben Quesada, Megan Stielstra, Ben Tanzer, and Lidia Yuknavitch.

All my love to Sandy Lee & Octavia Ortiz-Lee.

Wendy Ortiz is a self-taught mixed media artist from Los Angeles, California. Often somber and surreal, her work reflects a thoughtful melancholy in feminine form. Follow Wendy on Instagram for regular updates of her latest work (wendyortizart), and visit wendyortizart.com.

Wendy C. Ortiz is the author of *Excavation: A Memoir* (Future Tense Books, 2014) and *Hollywood Notebook* (Writ Large Press, 2015). Her work has been profiled or featured in the *Los Angeles Times*, the *Los Angeles Review of Books*, *The Rumpus*, and the National Book Critics Circle Small Press Spotlight blog. Her writing has appeared in such places as *The New York Times*, *Hazlitt*, *Vol. 1 Brooklyn*, *The Nervous Breakdown*, and a year-long series appeared at *McSweeney's Internet Tendency*. Wendy lives in Los Angeles. Visit wendyortiz.com & her public notebook at wendycortiz.tumblr.com.

OFFICIAL

CCM ◗

GET OUT OF JAIL
* VOUCHER *

- -

Tear this out.

Skip that social event.

It's okay.

You don't have to go if you don't want to. Pick up
the book you just bought. Open to the first page.
You'll thank us by the third paragraph.

If friends ask why you were a no-show, show them
this voucher.

You'll be fine.

- -

We're coping.

◗

CPSIA information can be obtained
at www.ICGtesting.com
Printed in the USA
LVHW040545240222
711836LV00007B/1218